Like a Fire Praying for Rain

SJ Duncan
Ink Ribbon Press

Like a Fire Praying for Rain: Copyright 2018 by SJ Duncan. All rights reserved. Printed in the United States of America. No part of this book may be used or reproduced in any manner whatsoever without written permission except in the case of brief excerpts embodied in critical articles and reviews. For information contact Ink Ribbon Press at irp@inkribbonpress.com.

First Ink Ribbon Press trade paperback edition: 2018

Your support of the author and authors' rights is appreciated.

For information about the author visit
www.sjduncan.com

Ink Ribbon Press is a division of Ink Ribbon Media. For information about bulk purchasing, events, or appearances, contact Ink Ribbon Press at
www.inkribbonpress.com

All Rights Reserved.

ISBN: 069208195X

ISBN-13: 978-0692081952

This is dedicated
to John and Dora Duncan
who gave me
my first typewriter
and a
fierce
entrepreneurial
spirit

Also by SJ Duncan

Novels

Bash
One in the Barrelhouse

Collected Poems

Like a Fire Praying for Rain
Three Rights and a Left
The Long Dark Lonesome

Contents

Taking a Break	3
Plucking and Pecking	4
Burning Boy Blue	6
Illustration	7
You Are Home	8
Quietly	9
Linger	10
The Spirits Get Restless Sometimes	11
Illustration	13
The Lost Men of Mountain Town	14
Hotel Living	16
Illustration	17
Like a Fire Praying for Rain	18
Ignition	19
Always Kinda	20
Swallowed Up and Spit Back Out	21
Illustration	23
This Kid I Know	24
Hotel Living II	26
Illustration	27
Potential	28
Slow-Motion Explosion	29
Illustration	31
Mr. Fixit for the Fifteenth Time	32
Mentorium	34
Hastings	35
Illustration	39
Indecency	40
Brick Walls and Icy Hot	41

Circles	42
Illustration	43
Hotel Living III	44
Socks	45
In Love with Being in Love with You	47
Saturday at the Hair Salon	48
The Bliss of Sleeping Dogs	49
The Current Rate of Inflation	51
Apples	53
Illustration	54
Hotel Living IV	55
Crumble	56
October 18th	58
Illustration	59
October 18th II	60
Graffiti Whitewash	61
Hinges	62
Illustration	63
Candles	64
Fully Formed	65
Illustration	67
Thousand-Yard Stare	68
Press Repeat	70
Hotel Living V	71
Just a Few Scratches	73
Note to Self	74
Cornered	76
Illustration	77
When Burning Boy Blue Burns Out	78
Hotel Leaving	79

Catch on fire and people will come
for miles to see you burn.

— John Wesley

Taking a Break

I told her
I would take a break
through Christmas
until New Year's
I wouldn't write
or plot
or scheme up ways
to get my words
out of my head
and on the page
I told her
I would take a break
but the fire inside
is too hot
and like a man on fire
I run
I run
leaving
hot
orange
sparks
in my wake
so when I say
I'm taking a break
what I really mean is
I'm suppressing
an impulse
for a day
or two
or a few
but never for long.

Plucking and Pecking

She sits on the floor
plucking notes from the keyboard
while I draw circles
on a sketch pad
trying to capture this thing
that's in the air
and failing
to pin it
down.

I was alone once
for a long time
and never said a word
keeping to myself
and capturing
stale air
and old arguments
a still life
of stagnation.

Today I'm an artist
tomorrow a musician
most days a writer
and on occasion
nothing at all
but a
still
quiet
man
with too much
on his mind.

Like a Fire Praying for Rain

She has fun
with the keyboard
sounding out songs
we both know.
She taught me
to speak
stand straight
listen...

I often have
too much on my mind
and she listens
like she hasn't
heard this
before
the same old arguments
bantered about
on stale air
in still rooms.

She listens
and plucks notes from the keyboard
while I try to capture
this thing in the air
trying too hard
and making too much noise
in my own head
plucking strange sounds
from imaginary problems
and pecking at
all the
wrong
keys.

Burning Boy Blue

Burning Boy Blue
knows what he knows
but knows there's more

He's hot inside
sweating
in damp discomfort
tight and itchy
like a sweater you can't take off
no matter how warm it gets
ice water please
and a fan
a fan
lots of fans
to cool this thing down

type
type
type
scribble
scribble

Burning Boy Blue
only knows
what keeps him straight
cool
calm
collected
and on fire
every moment
of every day

Like a Fire Praying for Rain

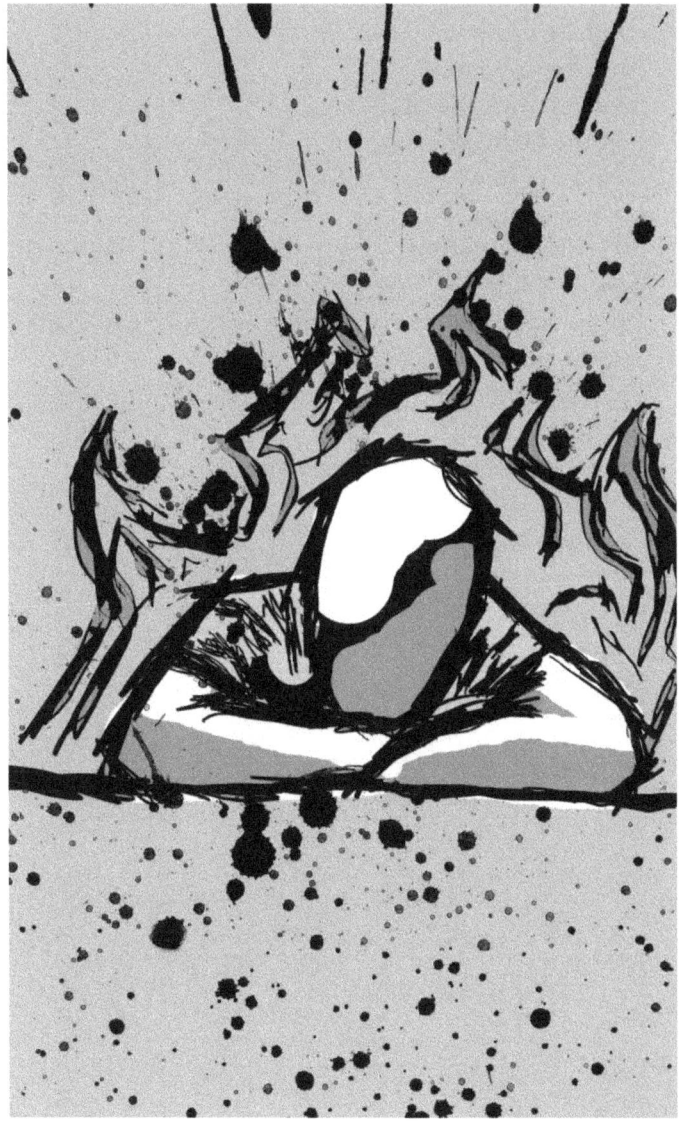

You Are Home

you are candy
you are solid gold
you are rock n' roll
on the highway
windows down
cruise control
you are a sunbeam
on a cool day
and a fresh breeze
to my summer heat
you are coffee
in the morning
and a comfortable place to sleep
and if I had to say it simply
I would say
you
are
home
to
me

Quietly

Some mornings
you wake
hours earlier
than you need to
and if there are still people
in the house
if you haven't
run them off
with your madness
if there are still people
who love you
living with you
then you step softly
through the dark
to the kitchen
where you
(quietly)
start the coffee
and
(quietly)
talk to the dog
and then you sit
(quietly)
in a still
calm
room
drinking coffee
scribbling prose
and waiting for
the people you love
to catch up

Linger

She puts her hands
on my face
and talks me down
when it gets bad
when it gets so bad
I can't see
any good way out
she touches me
and speaks life
and I live
for a while longer
her touch
lingers
and
so
do
I

The Spirits Get Restless Sometimes

The spirits get restless sometimes
and spoil good milk
and spill things
and when you're not looking
they take books down
from the shelf
and put them
where you'll never find them
and sometimes
they get your debit card
and order too much stuff
and then
when the stuff arrives
they leave empty boxes
and craft paper
on the coffee table
and spend the rest
of the afternoon
playing with their knickknacks.

Sometimes
you have to conduct a séance
to put them in their place
or send them back
to wherever they're from
but once they know you know
about them
they tell the others
and there you go.

They never put
toilet paper on the roller

or take the trash out
they don't walk the dog
pay bills
or wash dishes
and I've never seen one
mow the yard
but when it comes to messing up stuff
and wasting time
they're all over it.

The spirits get restless sometimes
and paint
write
sing
scream
sit on the floor
against the wall
draw shapes in the dust
on the window sill
and wish they weren't here
or anywhere at all
and it's then
after all the chaos that came before
that you start to feel
a little sorry
for them.

Like a Fire Praying for Rain

SJ Duncan

The Lost Men of Mountain Town

We arrived to find
lost men
begging for change
and buying booze
at 6 AM
loitering
at gas stations
with gorgeous views
of craggy creeks
purple-hazed vistas
and sharp
snowy
peaks
ever lovely
ever
out
of
reach.

I drove her into the mountains
that afternoon
and left her
at the women's retreat
here's your suitcase
I love you
my sweet
and she went into a grand hall
full of women
greeting one another
in a clean
bright
space

Like a Fire Praying for Rain

cheerful
and touched
by
deliberate
grace.

After that
I drove
back down the mountain
to sit in a hotel room
and write
lonely stories
in a town
filled with
lost men
begging for change
and buying booze
at 6 AM.

Hotel Living

Erase the agenda
sit in the room
stare at a wall
fidget with keys
autograph something
to leave for the maids
stand at the window
stare at the scene
shower forever
wipe away steam
sit on the bed
by the blank tv
check your inbox
let the phone ring
never call back
you don't have the time
think about smokes
and go to the door
step outside
and come right back in
then back to the desk
read what you've written
delete
repeat
again

Like a Fire Praying for Rain

Like a Fire Praying for Rain

I live with a dire love
burning hot and steady
flaring up
like
orange
paint
thrown against
the undercarriage
of the sky
this dire love
wanting something
I can never have
burning hot and fast
peeling layer after layer
only to find another
on and on
into infinity
living
like a man in agony
begging
like a dying willow
looking up
at the
hot
orange
undercarriage
of the sky
praying for relief
like a fire
praying for rain

Ignition

I spend my days
trying to go up in flames
douse the suit
climb on stage
and strike the match
(are you awake?)

More often
than I care to admit
the flame dwindles
before I can combust
a flash in the pan
a spark spiraling up
but I trust
the process
I trust

I spend my days
striking flint
against a wireless keyboard
over a blank document
keystroke
after keystroke
until something catches
and the
whole thing
goes
up

SJ Duncan

Always Kinda

i always kinda
lose myself
when the day's too nice
to be inside
or things go well
for very long
i always kinda
fall back down
when i let
old thoughts
back inside
and i always kinda
get stuck in ruts
spinning like tires
flinging mud
but i always kinda
find my peace
with
you
right
here
with
me

Swallowed Up and Spit Back Out

I'm fluent
in sarcasm
and snide remarks
overspending
becomes a way of life
there's never any jam
or jelly
for toast
and the neighbors know
I don't care about mowing
when I'm working
on a new book.

God told Jonah
to go to Nineveh
but Jonah was reluctant
now I digress.

The desk is full
of scribbles and notes
manuscripts
and blue and red pens.
The red ones are angry
the blue ones are sad
and I wonder
who's to blame.

I run like Jonah
and stow away
on cargo ships
hiding from fate
until God starts

tossing the sea
as I hunker down
in the hull
wasting days
wasting away
instead of being
where I'm
supposed to be
Nineveh
awaits.

The sea gets rough
and writing becomes
a raft on dark waters
at the edge of night
writing in the gloom
because it's the only way
I know
to survive.

The madness will
swallow you whole
if you let it
like the whale
did
Jonah.

When it
spits me up
on shore
at least I'll have
another book
to show for it.

Like a Fire Praying for Rain

This Kid I Know

He tells me
he wants it
so bad
he wants
the accolades
and acknowledgment
the fans
and the fame
the money
and the estate
and the headlines
newspaper clippings
awards
and most of all
he wants to be *known*
and if I told him the truth
he would turn away
if I told him the truth
about what it takes
what you have to overcome
sacrifice
and invest
before you ever see a return
if I told him the truth
about how many years
it usually takes
and how many bad books
you have to write
before you write
a good one
if I told him the truth
that love is the only thing

Like a Fire Praying for Rain

that can get you through this
that you have to love it
and need it
and have it
just to feel okay
if I told him the truth
about all that
he would realize
he doesn't want to be a writer
he just wants to be
rich and famous
and if being
rich and famous
is what he's after
there are much better ways
to go about it
than
this.

Hotel Living II

the bed is too big
without you in it
and the only reason
I get any sleep
is when the lack
catches up to me
and when that happens
my sleep is long and dark
and when that happens
I don't dream
which is good
because otherwise
I might dream
of a bed too big
in a room too lonely

Like a Fire Praying for Rain

Potential

It's cool
but not dark
bright
but not hot
and there's a lot
of potential
in the air
drifting around
ready to be made
into something
like stacks of lumber
bricks
and clay
handfuls of putty
jars of paint
and blank sheets of paper
stacked in reams
or maybe just
people
with
dreams

Slow-Motion Explosion

i pulled the pin
on a grenade
and held it
at arm's length
turning my face
and plugging one ear
waiting
for the big

KA-BANG!!!

it comes down to
energy transfer
how quickly
or slowly
you transition
from one state
to another
and the faster
the rate
the more violent
the change

caught in a
slow-motion explosion
there's plenty of time
to catch shrapnel
wondering
if i've done the right thing
by pulling the pin
wondering
if it's too late

to put it back in
knowing it's too late
now

if given the chance
i would
do it again

that sound
that sound
that
> *violent*
> *concussive*
> *blast*

is
how
i
feel
inside

you can't keep that in

Like a Fire Praying for Rain

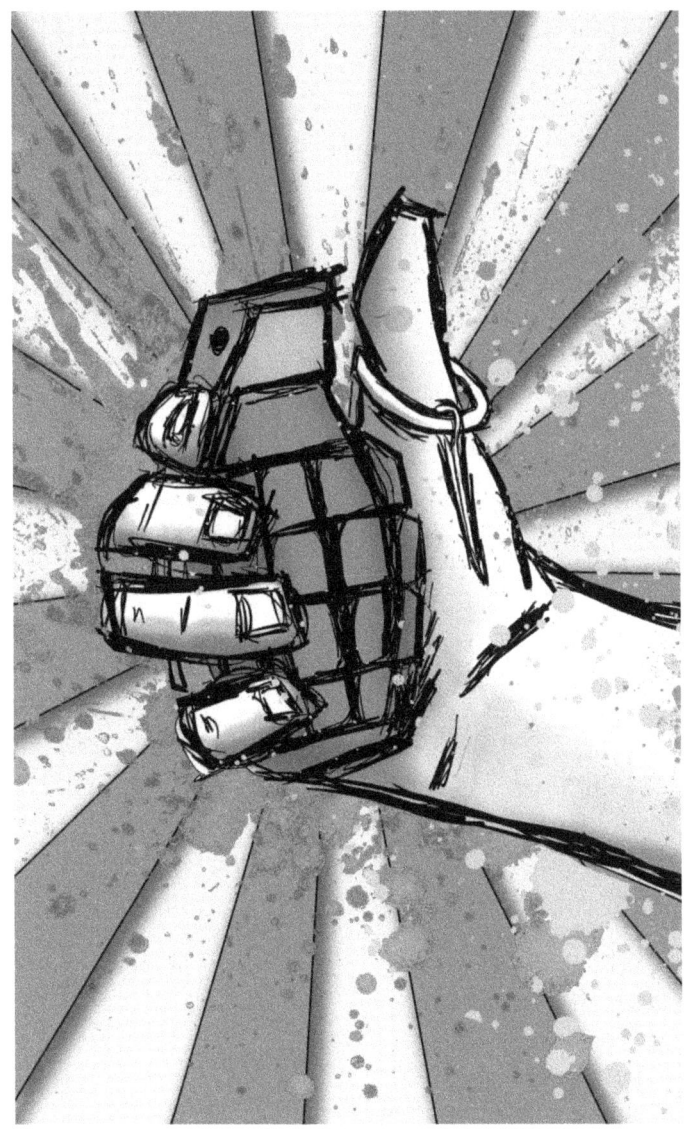

Mr. Fixit for the Fifteenth Time

Mom would read
to my sister
and me
at night
before tucking us in
kisses
> *I love you.*
> *Sweet dreams.*

We always begged
for one more story
one more book
one more time
> *This one again?*
> *Yes, that one again.*
and she obliged
pouring into us
words
thoughts
ideas
values
and the poetry
of life.

She was probably tired
most of those nights
and worried
about money
bills
our wellbeing
and the creeping flames
of passing time

and some nights
some dark
terrible
nights
she was probably broken hearted
but we never knew
these things.

Tired or not
she read to us
and we would ask
for one more
or the same book again
and she would read
one more
or the same book again
before putting us to bed
to dream
with a child's understanding
of our mother
fixing everything
including broken hearts.

SJ Duncan

Mentorium

They look to me
like I know the path
the ones who want
what little I've got
but don't know
where
to
start.

What I tell them is
I'm still finding my way
working it out daily
through
blind
dumb
faith
and never knowing
if I'm doing it right
just doing it
any
damn
way.

Hastings

The liquidation sale
goes on and on
like moths in a wardrobe
eating away
like a cancer
day
by
day.

It's hard to watch
this slow death
another share
of your youth
going away
not all at once
but piece by piece
20 percent off
then 30
now 40
slowly
over the course of weeks.

As a kid
you sat on the floor
reading *Where the Sidewalk Ends*
and later
as a teen
you shoplifted some things
and felt bad about it
but you learned so much
between these shelves

all the great works
and the new stuff, too,
the ones your friends
said you should read
and the ones you found
when you were
lost
lonely
in need.

40 percent off
now 50
now 60
and the furniture is for sale
the shelves are for sale
the coffee maker
the cash register
and everything else.

Throughout your twenties
you envied the authors
on these shelves
until finally
in your thirties
you became one
sitting behind a table
just over there
signing books
for the hometown crowd
proud and eager
to greet you
the way things must be
when you get to Heaven.

Like a Fire Praying for Rain

The liquidation sale
goes on and on
and strangers part around you
with armloads
of great finds
at incredible prices
unaware that once
not so long ago
you signed books
right
over
there.

60 percent
now 75
now 90
and everything must go
by Wednesday.

In *Fiction*
you find
one last copy
of your first novel
right there
amongst the greats.

This place made you
as much as any
in this small town
east of Dallas
and a long long way
from those publishers
in New York.

SJ Duncan

You don't buy any books.
You stack them neatly on the floor
and buy the shelf
not knowing where you'll put it
only that someday
you'll find a use for it
like all that stuff you learned
as a kid
sitting on the carpet
back there
in that empty space.

Like a Fire Praying for Rain

Indecency

Time is a bastard
and a poor guide
walking ahead
on treacherous paths
and never glancing back
to see if
you're keeping up
never acknowledging
complaints
or cries
and never caring
that you've twisted an ankle
or fallen behind
time moves on
and when you finally catch up
and shout in its face
it doesn't even have
the decency
to look you
in the
eye.

Brick Walls and Icy Hot

the lack of sleep
is getting to me
and this pulled muscle
in my shoulder
isn't helping
but if you never
run up against
your limitations
then
you
aren't
working
hard
enough

Circles

When you're not here
my life devolves into
pacing
and leaving trash behind
like a trail
here a coffee cup
a candy wrapper
some wadded-up pages
of writing that didn't work
like breadcrumbs
leading me back
into anxious circles
but never out
of my own mess
pacing the floor
in spirals of
missing you
spirals drawing tighter
until I'm spinning
now dizzy
on the floor
staring at the ceiling
sick of it all

Like a Fire Praying for Rain

Hotel Living III

when you aren't here
I don't want to
read
sleep
eat
hit the town
write the new book
or
even
finish
this

Socks

I get up early
on a Sunday
to get some writing done
before the kids wake
just me and the little dog
and some coffee
and this
but I don't get much done
before our youngest
comes around the corner
and stands by the desk
and asks what I'm working on
and I give him
the child-sized version
of the new book
and he nods
but I know
it's not his kind of story
and then he asks
if I can help him find some socks
so I ask
if he needs them right this minute
and he says his feet are cold
so we get up
and dig through the dryer
and find some socks
and he's happy
and I'm happy
and even though
I don't get much writing done
this morning
I don't mind

because one day
I'll have all the time I want
to sit at the desk
and write books
and miss the days
when small people
interrupted a morning's work
asking for socks.

In Love with Being in Love with You

I fell in love today
with the way you
touch my back
when I'm down
and listen
when I go on and on
about something
that shouldn't be an issue
but is
I fell in love today
with the way you smile
and that new hairstyle
and the picture you posted
of you
in your car
after getting it cut
and I fell in love today
with living
in your good graces
and knowing you're there
to shout down the devils
I can't beat on my own
and I fell in love today
with being in love
with
you.

SJ Duncan

Saturday at the Hair Salon

I sit with your purse
across from a white Christmas tree
on a green upholstered bench
with sparkly pillows
watching the parking lot
through the window
tired
of staring at my phone.

Ladies come and go
What'll it be
I think I want it short
or colored
or curled
or feathered
maybe an ombre
and have you heard
what happened
and how?

I sit with your purse
on the green upholstered bench
on a cold Saturday
at the hair salon
and watch the parking lot
through the window
when I'm not looking
at my phone
or the Christmas tree
or the sparkly pillows.

Here, I am content.

The Bliss of Sleeping Dogs

the desk is littered
with scraps of paper
empty coffee mugs
and the worst
of the best
of intentions

the wood is worn
around the edges
and the drawers are full
of who-knows-what
and there are a lot
of pens

I have a job to do
so I show up
each morning
with a fresh cup of coffee
and the best of intentions
and some mornings
I earn my keep
while the little dog rests
at my feet
glancing up on occasion
but mostly
stretching
scratching
or getting herself
comfortable

she doesn't know
what it's like

SJ Duncan

to have a deadline
and a desk
littered
with the worst
of the best
of intentions

The Current Rate of Inflation

feeling like a tire
with a slow leak
waking each day
lower
closer to the ground
puncture wounds
counter
the current
rate
of
inflation

kiss me
babe
kiss me long and deep
and breath into me
your tender compassion
inhale my suffering
exhale your light

the leak is slow
we can do this all day
every hour
every minute
drive slow
better late
than not at all
we'll get there when we get there
pull over
drag out the air pump
wait for the tire to rise
speak life into me

speak fire into me
speak

slowly
and
carefully
we
go
down
the
road

Apples

I sang
the saddest song I knew
to my heart's discontent
spilling my soul
like the contents
of an
overturned
applecart
apples rolling
into the street
lost to the gutter
or squished
at speed
or gathered up
and carried off
to
places
unknown
for the hungry
to
eat.

Hotel Living IV

Adjust the tie
tug at the collar

pretend you're not anxious

comb your hair
check your teeth
and nostrils
in the mirror

pretend you're important

check the pens
check the markers
check to see
that your signature still swoops

pretend you're big time

put on the shoes
put on the jacket
put on airs
and pretend
you aren't the same guy
letting all that trash pile up
back at the hotel

Crumble

The house
crumbles around us
bits of
drywall
and splintered studs
shingles
trim and baseboards
all of it
coming down
in one
magnificent
cataclysmic
puff.

What do you want for dinner?
She asks
I don't care, you pick,
and she says chicken
but we've had chicken
twice this week
Maybe that new place?
That's fine with me.
so we leave the house
in a heap of rubble
and we have a nice meal
at that new place
and no chicken.

Later
we crawl through debris
to the couch
to cuddle

and play on our phones
and when it's time for bed
I move a section of wall for her
and she calls me
her strong man
and when we hit the bed
dust billows into the air.

I miss the roof
she says in the dark
and I agree
drawing her close.
It's supposed to rain tomorrow
she says
I know
I whisper
and she asks what we'll do with no roof.

Get wet, I suppose,
is all I can say.

October 18th

today
i wrote
one
shitty
throwaway
poem
about
nothing

Like a Fire Praying for Rain

October 18th Part II

one?

Graffiti Whitewash

Sometimes
you come across a memory
so sudden
and unexpected
it takes something
out of you
something more
than your wind
something escaping
from your core
through
a jagged hole
you thought
had healed
long
ago

she wrote
I love you
on the door
in permanent marker
but I
was
already
gone

Hinges

The hinges started squeaking again
so we oiled them
and that made things better
for a time

She touches my face
and says
> *I love you*
> *I need you here*

and I tell her I know
and promise
that I'm not going anywhere
> *I'll stay*
> *I'll stay*

The hinges squeak
now and again
and when it gets
too bad
for
too long
we oil them
and work the door
and things get better
for a time

I stay
even when I don't want too
even when the squeaking becomes a scream
even when there's no oil left in the bottle

> *I love you so*

Like a Fire Praying for Rain

Candles

Maybe we burn
because we're careless
or because
life is a fire
and we're frail
combustible
like dry grass and wicker
maybe because
we touch hot things
even though
we've learned that lesson before
or maybe because
we deserve it
or think we do
or maybe because
we're candles
in the darkness
and others
need the light.

Fully Formed

I used to admire them
writers
this one
for the plot
even if the prose was plain
or that one
for his
portrayal of the south
or another
for the longing
in her poetry
I used to admire them
until I became one
fully formed
and hardened in the mold
typing out
a sickness
I can't shake
a sickness
that subsides
abates
then flairs once more
until I burn
with that same old fever
failing
to get it all down
failing
to get it right
I burn
and fail
and fall short of greatness
no matter how much

SJ Duncan

time I take
and I no longer
admire writers
because I know them
and I know
the sickness
all too well
I know them
and the heat in that fever
and I no longer admire writers
I pity us
the whole crazy bunch

Like a Fire Praying for Rain

SJ Duncan

Thousand-Yard Stare

The ones who make it
have this look
call it a *thousand-yard stare*
or whatever
but you know it when you see it
and you know
they know something
you don't

all the time
some kid comes up to me
some kid wanting desperately
to be a writer
some kid who thinks
that if his words are
smart enough
or clever enough
or eloquent enough
or angry enough
or *edgy* enough
that the great golden gates
of writerdom
will swing wide
and let him in
and I listen
and offer what advice I have
from what I've known
but I don't tell him
what I think

what I think is
the ones who make it

Like a Fire Praying for Rain

have this look
this *thousand-yard stare*
hard earned
like rough hands
calloused
from years of hard work
and that it doesn't matter how
smart
or clever
or eloquent
or angry
or edgy
the words are
as long
as they
speak
truth

Press Repeat

Eventually
you circle around
to where you were before
doing what you did
but differently
if you're smarter
and better
if you're crafty
diligent
and determined
if you're blessed enough
to have passed
through the fiery furnace
enough times
to become tempered
and refined
and pure
and holy
and whole
even if it takes some time
because eventually you wrap around
to where you were before
the circle closes
the curve is round
and it all
starts
to
make
sense

Hotel Living V

Turn up the music
dance to the desk
write

stop to think
stop to breathe
go to the balcony
spit over the rail
on the asphalt below
formulate a plot
consider character arc
dance to the desk
write

stop for coffee
stop to think
consider pacing
theme
and the possibility
you're trying too hard

slow and steady
wins the race

go outside
circle the pool
don't smoke because you quit
catch a glimpse
of inspiration
hurry to the room
write

turn up the music
turn up the heat
hunch over
lean in
and don't forget
to breathe
as you
find your voice
find your angle
find your way
down a long dark trail
with a tiny flashlight
throw words at the wall
to see what sticks
and leave the rest
on the floor
for housekeeping

Just a Few Scratches

Somewhere along the way
I ripped my jeans
burned a hole
in my shirt
and lost the sole
of one shoe.

The elbows got a little
scuffed up
from all the crawling
and I snagged my shirt
on barbed wire
at least a dozen times.

I lost track of the miles
somewhere along the way
and started over at zero
and eventually
lost track again
and stopped counting
then.

It's been a long walk
with a lot of baggage
but to arrive
with just a few scratches
and one throbbing shoulder
I'd say
I'm doing pretty well.

SJ Duncan

Note to Self

Don't confuse
a thing that happened
with poetry

waiting on buses
or riding in subways
or sitting in hotel rooms
pretending to be
a better writer
than you are

don't confuse
waking up and going back to sleep
and maybe getting drunk
or hitting the town
or losing half your money
on a bad bet
don't confuse
these things
with poetry

don't confuse
a bad date
a bad day
a bad week
a bad year
or a bad lifetime
with poetry

don't confuse
starving
crying

Like a Fire Praying for Rain

dying
winning
losing
admiring
longing
loving
leaving
or running late again
with poetry
and don't confuse
a thing that happened
with a thing
that has meaning

the sun sets every day
but not always
while your heart
is breaking

Cornered

It gets lonely
as the day goes on
and the light comes in
sideways
through the windows
too soft
too faded
too much and not enough.

It isn't sufficient
to keep yourself occupied
during the day
because night always follows
and when you run out of
things to do
that's when you
run
out
of
room.

It's not a good way to be
feeling cornered
with the light
coming in sideways
like that.

It kinda makes you
rethink
the way
you spent your day.

Like a Fire Praying for Rain

SJ Duncan

When Burning Boy Blue Burns Out

when the rains come
and the
fire
smolders out
don't cry
or worry
or fear for me
just know
I was born
a raging inferno
and I burned
my whole life long
hot
and bright
and anguished
screaming
one keystroke
at a time
and pleading
for something
to simply
put
me
out

Hotel Leaving

You're probably forgetting
the cord to the laptop
your toothbrush
maybe the keys to the car
parked at an airport
a thousand miles away
the credit card
or your phone
and you'll probably
remember what it is
when you're 30,000 feet in the air
politely declining
the peanuts
and staring down
at the tops of clouds

writing is a
beautiful terror
a magnificent melancholic
wonderland
full of
love
laughter
and teeth

they sell more of them
whatever it is you're forgetting
and in the end
nothing matters anyway
but the love you gave
and the purpose you served
and if it makes you feel

SJ Duncan

any better
you also
forgot
to shave

writing is a
blood sport
like picking berries
in a briar patch
you bleed
but the berries
are sweet

it can be as easy
or hard
as you make it
take your time
be deliberate
diversify
and
oblige

whatever it is
you're forgetting
will be forgotten in the end
ashes to ashes
dust to dust
the sum
of a million
inconsequential
bubble
bursts

Like a Fire Praying for Rain

writing is a
splendid diversion
like a tumble
down a well
self-hypnosis
fine dining
in a mirror maze
with a toast
to
yourself

ad infinitum
ad nauseum

you're probably forgetting
something
and that's okay
because you're doing
in this life
what you came to do
and how many
can say
the
same?

About the Author

SJ Duncan is an author, ghostwriter, public speaker, and musician. He collects old typewriters, dabbles in photography, and was once a member of a CCR tribute band. He lives in North Texas with his wife, children, dog, and the old typewriters.

For more information visit
www.sjduncan.com

www.ingramcontent.com/pod-product-compliance
Lightning Source LLC
Chambersburg PA
CBHW032022040426
42448CB00006B/710